Bev Aisbett is the author  highly regarded self-help texts for sufferers of anxiety and depression, most notably *Living with IT* and *Taming the Black Dog*. These books are distributed to health professionals nationwide and have been translated into four languages.

A trained counsellor, Bev is also the facilitator of the 'Working with IT' recovery program in Melbourne and assists those in other states through 'THE IT KIT', a home study version of the workshop. She conducts lectures to assist sufferers of depression and anxiety within metropolitan and regional Victoria.

Bev is also a recognised artist and her soulful paintings are regularly exhibited in Melbourne and Tasmania.

Workshop and lecture information: www.adavic.org
IT Kit information: www.bevaisbett.com

ALSO BY BEV AISBETT

The Book of IT
Fixing IT
Taming the Black Dog
Get Real
Letting IT Go
Living IT Up
Recovery: A Journey to Healing
The Little Book of IT
I Love Me

GET OVER IT!

How to stop being a VICTIM of the PAST

HarperCollins*Publishers*

HarperCollins*Publishers*

First published in Australia in 2010
by HarperCollins*Publishers* Australia Pty Limited
ABN 36 009 913 517
harpercollins.com.au

Copyright © Bev Aisbett 2010

The right of Bev Aisbett to be identified as the author
and illustrator of this work has been asserted by her
under the *Copyright Amendment (Moral Rights) Act 2000*.

This work is copyright. Apart from any use as permitted under the
Copyright Act 1968, no part may be reproduced, copied, scanned, stored
in a retrieval system, recorded, or transmitted, in any form or by any
means, without the prior written permission of the publisher.

HarperCollins*Publishers*
Level 13, 201 Elizabeth Street, Sydney, NSW 2000, Australia
31 View Road, Glenfield, Auckland 0627, New Zealand
A 53, Sector 57, Noida, UP, India
77–85 Fulham Palace Road, London, W6 8JB, United Kingdom
2 Bloor Street East, 20th floor, Toronto, Ontario M4W 1A8, Canada
10 East 53rd Street, New York NY 10022, USA

National Library of Australia Cataloguing-in-Publication data:

Aisbett, Bev.
   Get over it!/Bev Aisbett.
   ISBN 978 0 7322 9117 4 (pbk.).
   Depression, Mental. Stress (Psychology)
   616.8527

Cover and internal illustrations by Bev Aisbett
Typeset in 13pt Comic Sans by Kirby Jones
Printed and bound in Australia by Griffin Press
50gsm Bulky News used by HarperCollins*Publishers* is a natural, recyclable product
made from wood grown in sustainable plantation forests. The manufacturing processes
conform to the environmental regulations in the country of origin, New Zealand.

5 4 3 2   11 12 13

DEDICATION

To my parents,
Millicent and Arthur.
Long gone, released with love
but never forgotten.

CONTENTS

INTRODUCTION	9
DO NOT PASS GO	11
HOLDING OURSELVES HOSTAGE	31
THE PRISONER AS VICTIM	47
VICTIM SUPPORT	61
IT WASN'T ME	71
FOR BETTER OR WORSE	83
PLANNING THE ESCAPE ROUTE	103
BREAKING FREE	113
RELEASING THE VICTIM	139

INTRODUCTION

Yes, I hear you. You've been hurt badly. Things have been tough from the very start. Life just seemed to throw it at you ... challenge after challenge, so many you hardly recovered from one before there was another!

God knows, I've had more than my fair share too. (It's all part of my research!)

And, just like you, I have at times lamented my lot, raged at the unfairness of things and blamed all and sundry (including God!) for placing me in painful situations.

That is, until I knew better.

If you feel that life has been unfair to you, through no fault of your own, this book will challenge you.

I make no apologies for that.

My aim is to empower you to free yourself from the prison of the past.

Of course, you will need to be WILLING to do that.

If you are, take a deep breath,
be brave, be honest ... and be free.

DO NOT PASS GO

Go on, tell me your story.

Didn't anything **GOOD** happen?

Have you noticed that if you ask most people their history they will usually come up with their **Miseryography**? A life story filled with **SADNESS, HURT, ANGER** and **REGRET**: this will tend to override even the **BEST** of times in their memory.

Get two people discussing their past and invariably they will get into a strange form of 'oneupmanship', where they actually **COMPETE** for who has had the greatest suffering!

The saying 'misery loves company' could not be more true.

Our society **THRIVES** on it ...

... and the Press would be downright **LOST** without it!

However, holding onto the trials of the past means waking up every day in a **PRISON** ...

... and for many people, it's this kind of **GROUNDHOG DAY** every day!

In fact, some prisoners of the past go so far as to **SACRIFICE** the things that they once **LOVED** doing because these things remind them of a time **LONG GONE** ...

... and, even worse, there are those who stay **STUCK IN SUFFERING** for **DECADES** because of a past wrongdoing, wanting the wrongdoer to somehow make it right, sometimes even if the wrongdoer **DIED YEARS AGO**!

ARE YOU A PRISONER OF THE PAST?

Let's take a look:

You expect the **WORST** because you believe you've failed before.

You are afraid to be **YOURSELF** because you have been previously **REJECTED**.

You fear **CRITICISM** because you have been **CRITICISED** before.

YOU'RE TOO THIS, TOO THAT & TOO EVERYTHING

You won't let others get **CLOSE** to you in case you are **HURT** again.

You feel **FEARFUL**, **ANXIOUS** or **DEPRESSED** most of the time because things were once so **PAINFUL**.

You see others as **AUTHORITY FIGURES** in your life, just as you did when you were a **CHILD**.

You are afraid to **SPEAK UP** or set **BOUNDARIES** in case you **OFFEND** and thus risk being **ABANDONED**.

You feel that life is **UNFAIR** and that others **LET YOU DOWN**.

You are easily **UPSET** by any number of others' **WORDS, GESTURES** and **ACTIONS** because they **TRIGGER** old hurts.

Your life tends to be one **CRISIS** after another.

If you are able to recognise yourself in the above examples, you are **HOLDING ONTO THE PAST** (and congratulations on your honesty).

Until we become **AWARE**, our **CURRENT IDENTITY** remains completely entwined with our **PAST STRUGGLES**.

Our **PAST** writes the script for our **PRESENT** experiences.

The past also dictates the **FUTURE**, based on our **EXPECTATIONS** ...

... which are also based on **PAST EXPERIENCES!**

However, many people who are holding onto their past believe that it is actually the **OTHER WAY** around!

The past can only have a **HOLD** over you if you keep **DRAGGING** it with you into every new experience. Freeing yourself from the prison of the past can be as simple as making a **DECISION** not to continue to do so.

To see how this can happen, let's take a look at the story of the **MONKEY TRAP**.

One day, two shamans (or medicine men) met for a conference.

One was a **NATIVE AMERICAN** and the other came from **AFRICA**.

As they compared notes on their various rituals and practices, the African shaman instructed his colleague on the art of **CATCHING A MONKEY**.

STEP 1:
Find a **PUMPKIN** and remove all the pulp till it is hollow.

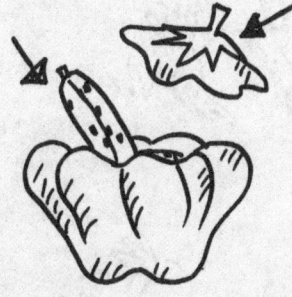

STEP 2:
Place a **BANANA** inside the hollow and seal it up again.

STEP 3:
Make a **HOLE** in the pumpkin that is just large enough for the monkey's forearm to fit through.

THE MONKEY TRAP IS NOW READY.

TRAPPING THE MONKEY

Here comes the **MONKEY** down the path.

Suddenly, he smells a familiar and irresistible aroma drifting from that **PUMPKIN**.

He reaches into the hole and seizes the **BANANA**.

(CUT-AWAY VIEW)

The monkey is now **TRAPPED!**

To **FREE** himself, all he needs do is **LET GO** of the **BANANA!**

... but instead, he blames the **PUMPKIN!**

IF IT WASN'T FOR THIS STUPID PUMPKIN I'D BE FREE!

29

The '**HOLD**' that the past has over us works in a similar way.

We think that we are **TRAPPED** by past circumstances but it is actually our **ATTACHMENT** to the old **MESSAGES**, **BELIEFS** and **CONDITIONING** that keeps us **STUCK**.

The same patterns endlessly **REPEAT** and we feel helpless to escape from them.

It is time to **BREAK FREE**.

HOLDING OURSELVES HOSTAGE

Of course, **MOVING ON** from the past can seem easier said than done. After all, the past frames virtually everything we **THINK**, **SAY** and **DO**.

It is undeniable that the past has had a huge influence on shaping the person you are today. Observe how **PAST BELIEFS** influence your **THOUGHTS, FEELINGS** and **ACTIONS** in the **PRESENT**:

From our earliest years, our primary focus is on having our **NEEDS** met. In childhood, our very **SURVIVAL** relied on this.

In order to **LIVE**, we needed to be **NURTURED**; and if we were not **ACCEPTED**, we did not **SURVIVE**.

To ensure that we received this essential **NURTURE, LOVE** or **APPROVAL**, we may have had to **BURY** certain aspects of ourselves which were deemed **UNACCEPTABLE** ...

... or **BRING FORWARD** more **PLEASING** aspects.

We may have had to create a **FALSE SELF** to compensate when our **TRUE SELF** was deemed to be less than **IDEAL**.

I'LL LOVE YOU IF YOU DO **THIS** & DON'T DO **THAT**!

Actually, we normally create **SEVERAL** false selves to serve our needs, protect us and ensure our **SURVIVAL**.

These **FALSE SELVES** are like characters in a play, each **TRIGGERED** by the current script but initially **CREATED** through the dramas of the past.

HOW DID I GET **HERE**?

I PROMPTED YOU!

We interpret **CURRENT SITUATIONS** through the filter of our own **HISTORY**. We **REACT** to **CURRENT** situations ...

... depending on whether the current event triggers memories of feeling similar emotions in the **PAST**.

If the emotional '**CHARGE**' associated with a previous event is strong, we will tend to 'act out' and the **FALSE SELF** that was once hidden will present itself again.

Let's look at an example of how this works.

Meet **GODFREY THE GOOD GUY**.

Godfrey loves keeping people happy. He is always **PLEASANT**, **POLITE** and goes out of his way to be **HELPFUL**.

That is, until people take advantage of his **GENEROSITY** once too often.

Suddenly, gentle **GODFREY** erupts in furious tirade:

DO YOUR OWN DISHES!!

This is so unlike Godfrey! He's normally so **MILD** and **FRIENDLY**!

WHAT'S WITH GODFREY?

YEAH, THAT WAS SO OUT OF CHARACTER!

Indeed, Godfrey, *is* **OUT OF CHARACTER!** He has flipped over into his alter ego, **TERRY THE TYRANT!**

GODFREY initially created the **GOOD GUY** character out of a fear of **CONFLICT**.

(He did this because his aggressive father constantly **BERATED** him as a child.)

By being **ACCOMMODATING** he hoped to avoid being on the receiving end of similar **AGGRESSION** from others ...

... but in doing so, he also knew that he was perceived as **WEAK** and despised himself for it.

This inner loathing remained hidden until he was shown his own **WEAKNESS** one too **MANY TIMES** ...

HAPPY BIRTHDAY, GODFREY!

... which triggered him into reacting with the **SAME BEHAVIOUR** he had so despised in his father.

OH NO! I LOST IT! I'M SO ASHAMED!

People who are stuck in acting out from the past will often swing between two **EXTREMES**. The pressures of playing a particular role become too great and they will subsequently **FLIP** into the opposite behaviour.

Let's see a few examples of these dual roles.

Introducing:
THE FABULOUS FALSE SELF SHOW! FEATURING ...

"HAPPY TO HELP!"

"AS LONG AS IT'S MY WAY."

HILARY HELPFUL, who also plays **CARLA CONTROLLER**

LIFE'S A BALL!

EXCEPT MY LIFE.

PHIL FUNSTER, who also plays **DAN DOWNER**

I'M SURE TO GET PROMOTED! and **BUT I'LL PROBABLY GET PASSED OVER.**

GARRY GO-GETTER, who also plays **SAM SELF-DOUBTER**

And so the list goes on. In fact there could be a cast of **THOUSANDS**.

Can you **IDENTIFY** and **NAME** some of your own characters?

The main things that all these characters have in **COMMON** are:

None is fully **ADULT**

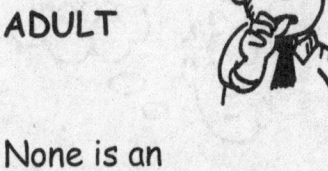

None is an **AUTHENTIC SELF**

I HATE WHO I AM!

Each has a sense of **SELF-LOATHING**

All have been created by the **PAST**!

It is as if we are tethered to a pendulum which swings between **SHAME** and **BLAME**.

SHAME   *BLAME*

The character we created to **ESCAPE** certain emotions becomes the character that **IMPRISONS** us.

I'LL BE GOOD!

HAVE TO BE BETTER!

When we try to cut loose from these confines, we find ourselves back in the emotional place that we were trying to **AVOID** in the first place!

I'VE BEEN BAD!

As a result, we find ourselves feeling **OUT OF CONTROL** and **POWERLESS** in our own lives.

I'VE BLOWN IT AGAIN!

We **KNOW** we overreact
but can't seem to stop it.

> I AM **NOT** OVERLY SENSITIVE!

We swing from one **DRAMA** to the next
without knowing **WHY**.

> HOW ARE THINGS? NO, WAIT ... DON'T ANSWER THAT!

And worst of all, we find
ourselves
locked into the **LEAD ROLE**:

the
VICTIM

THE PRISONER AS VICTIM

The false self or character most responsible for your ongoing imprisonment is the **VICTIM**.

Few people would like to admit it, but most of us have played the role of the **VICTIM** at some stage.

You'll know that you're playing the **VICTIM** character if you feel:

HELPLESS

WHAT TO DO?

DISEMPOWERED

YIKES!

IMMOBILISED

TOO HARD!

FEARFUL

TOO SCARY!

TAKEN FOR GRANTED

"WASH THESE!"

REGRETFUL

"IF ONLY..."

RESENTFUL

RESIGNED

"IT'S NO USE TRYING!"

and, let's be very honest now ...

SELF-PITYING

"WOE IS ME."

In fact, you can't really be the **VICTIM** without feeling **SORRY** for yourself! It goes with the territory! So, just for now, without judgement, **NOTICE** when you are doing this.

The **VICTIM** thinks:

Life should be **FAIR** and **EASY**

> I TRIED **SO** HARD! THEY SHOULD HAVE HIRED ME!

People should **LOVE ME** no matter what I **DO**

If I'm **GOOD**, good things will **FOLLOW**

> AFTER ALL I DID IT FOR THEM!

People shouldn't **CRITICISE** me or **DISAGREE** with me

> THEY'RE PICKING ON ME!

I should never be **SAD**, **LONELY**, **BROKE**, **HUNGRY**, **BORED** or **REJECTED**

BUT THAT'S WHAT A CREDIT CARD'S FOR!

OVER LIMIT

and, if I am, it just **HAPPENED** to me!

The world should **LOOK AFTER** me

LOANS

MONGREL BANKS!

and, if something goes wrong, it must be someone or something else's **FAULT** because it can't possibly be **MINE**!

THEY SHOULD HAVE STOPPED ME SPENDING!

The **VICTIM** tends to pop up frequently in **CONFLICT** situations, especially when we feel that we have been **TREATED UNFAIRLY** or **MISUNDERSTOOD**.

PEOPLE ARE MEAN TO ME!

For some people, being the **VICTIM** is the only way they have learned to engage with the world and have their **NEEDS** met.

HAVE YOU EVER BEEN HAPPY?

WHAT'S THAT?

Others may find themselves in situations in which the role of **VICTIM** has been **THRUST UPON** them through:

TRAUMA

LOSS

or **INJURY**.

No matter how one comes to find oneself in the role of **VICTIM**, the pain can be very **REAL** and **OVERWHELMING**.

It may even be **VALIDATED** by extreme circumstances.

Nonetheless, continuing to **HOLD ONTO PAIN** well after an event turns the **PAST** into a **PRISON**.

HOW LONG AGO DID YOU LOSE HIM?

WHEN I WAS SIX!

So, for now, let's just say yes, it **HURTS**, yes it was **AWFUL**, yes, it seems **UNFAIR** but here is the question:

DO YOU REALLY WANT TO STAY THERE?

> OF COURSE NOT! I'M SUFFERING!

You may **THINK** that you would rather **NOT** continue to feel this **BAD**, but when it comes to the crunch, you may actually **CHOOSE** to **STAY STUCK**.

The trouble with the **VICTIM** character is that it can actually become more **COMFORTABLE** to stay in **STRUGGLE** than to move out of it.

> OH, COME ON! WHY WOULD I DO THAT?

Because there are certain **BENEFITS** to be derived from remaining the **VICTIM**.

> BENEFITS? WHAT BENEFITS?

We need to explore some of these.

A victim is:

not **RESPONSIBLE**

ENTITLED to **SYMPATHY**

'SPECIAL'

MORALLY 'RIGHT'

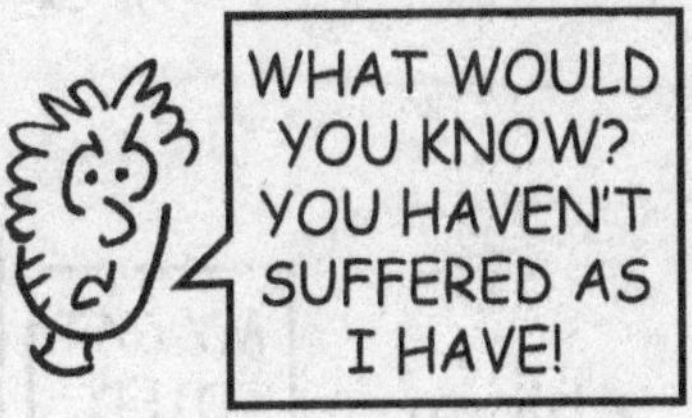

PROTECTED from **FURTHER HURT**

Able to **BLAME** outside factors

Able to excuse his or her **ACTING OUT**

LOOKED AFTER

BUT HE'S TROUBLED!

NO, HE'S TROUBLE!

I'VE MOWN YOUR LAWN, FIXED YOUR FENCE & DONE YOUR SHOPPING!

I'M NOT WELL! CAN YOU DO MY TAX?

Able to **BOND** with others through a shared **TRAUMA**

MY CAT DIED

SO DID MY BUDGIE!

AND MY GOLD FISH!

PET GRIEF GROUP

Somehow '**BAD**' or **DESERVING** of **PUNISHMENT**.

I HAVE TO DO PENANCE!

No matter how **DIFFICULT** it may be to move on, the result is the same: as the **VICTIM**, your wellbeing and sense of worth is governed by the **PAST, OTHERS** and **OUTSIDE FACTORS**.

Initially, **VICTIM** behaviours arise as a means of:

Getting **NEEDS** Met

I NEED YOU TO GIVE ME COMFORT & SUPPORT!

Handling **PAINFUL EMOTIONS**

I CAN'T DEAL WITH THIS ON MY OWN!

OR as a protective device or a way of gaining control.

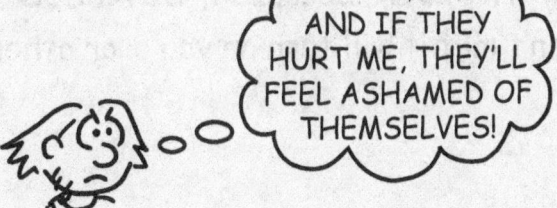

AND IF THEY HURT ME, THEY'LL FEEL ASHAMED OF THEMSELVES!

The problem is that the device which **PROTECTED** you from the pain of the past is now the very thing that keeps you locked to it.

As long as we seek, even unconsciously, to find '**REWARDS**' as a **VICTIM**, we remain **DISEMPOWERED**.

It is at this point that the **VICTIM** becomes the **TYRANT**, **BULLY** and **CONTROLLER**, because if its **NEEDS** aren't met it will turn on you ... or others.

VICTIM SUPPORT

If we take a look at the **VICTIM'S** attitudes, there is a common thread.

They are those of a **CHILD**.

The **VICTIM** is really the **WOUNDED CHILD** in us.

Be honest, how **OLD** are you when you are feeling:

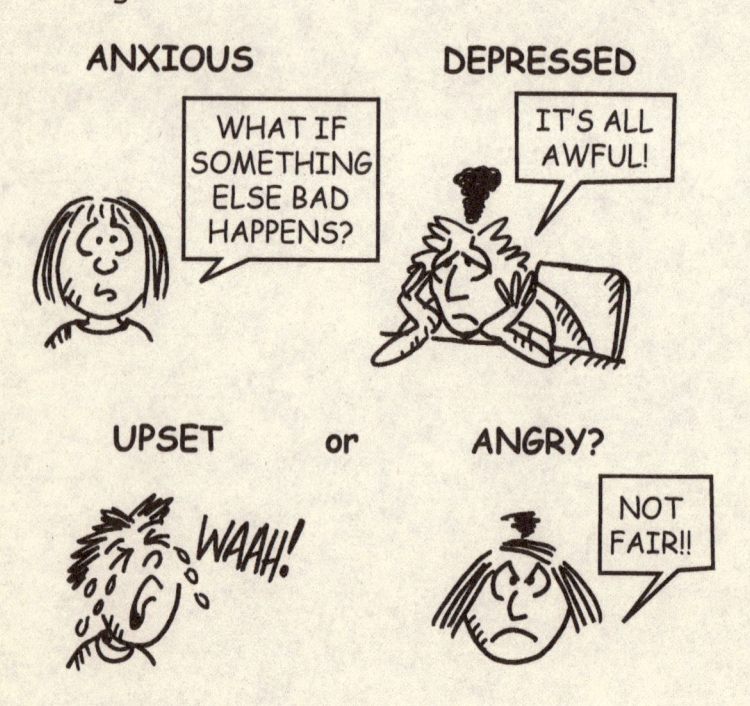

ANXIOUS

WHAT IF SOMETHING ELSE BAD HAPPENS?

DEPRESSED

IT'S ALL AWFUL!

UPSET or **ANGRY?**

WAAH!

NOT FAIR!!

If the **VICTIM** is the **CHILD** in you, then you will tend to expect:

THAT YOU SHOULD BE APPRECIATED

> I'VE DEDICATED MY LIFE TO MY ART! WHY ISN'T IT SELLING?

THAT EVERYONE CAN BE TRUSTED

> HE LIED TO ME AGAIN!

> SURPRISE, SURPRISE

THAT YOU WILL BE RESCUED

> STOP LETTING ME EAT SO MUCH!

THAT THE 'BIG PEOPLE' KNOW BEST

> WHY ARE YOU STILL TAKING THESE? THEY MAKE YOU WORSE!

> I MUST DO AS THE DOCTOR SAYS!

THAT LIFE SHOULD BE EASY

THAT BAD THINGS SHOULDN'T HAPPEN

THAT YOU CAN'T GET OVER IT

> MY LIFE'S OVER!

THAT YOU CAN'T SAY NO

> THEY'LL BE UPSET IF I REFUSE!

AND THAT YOU CAN'T HELP WHAT HAPPENS TO YOU.

> I'M JUST UNLUCKY!

And if the **VICTIM** is the child, then you would want the '**GROWN UPS**' to:

REASSURE YOU

- I'M WORRIED!
- IT WILL BE OK!

TAKE CONTROL

- I DON'T KNOW WHAT TO DO!
- I'LL FIX IT!

FIND A SOLUTION

- I'M IN SUCH TROUBLE!
- LEAVE IT WITH ME!

ACT IN YOUR BEST INTERESTS

- THEY CHEATED ME!
- SOMEONE SHOULD HAVE A WORD!

INTERVENE FOR YOU

- OH NO! I CAN'T FACE THEM!
- THEN I WILL!

PROTECT YOU

- WHAT IF THEY GET NASTY?
- I'LL LOOK AFTER YOU!

PUT IN THE HARD WORK

"I SIMPLY CAN'T COPE."

"THERE, THERE. YOU JUST REST!"

FACE UP TO DIFFICULTIES

"I'M NOT STRONG ENOUGH!"

"THAT'S WHY I'M HERE!"

KEEP YOU SHIELDED FROM UNPLEASANT THINGS

"IT'S TOO TERRIBLE!"

"YOU SHOULDN'T HAVE TO GO THROUGH THIS!"

WORRY ABOUT YOU

NO! NO! NO!

"I HATE SEEING YOU UPSET!"

All well and good ... if you are a **CHILD**!

And provided your **SUPPORT NETWORK** is willing to go along with this dynamic.

Of course, we **ALL** need help at times but what if others are **UNABLE** or **UNWILLING** to help you through?

WHERE'S MY WHITE KNIGHT?

What if your **NEEDS** can't be met and you find yourself having to cope **ALONE**?

If you have placed your whole **WELLBEING** into the hands of **OTHERS**, the **VICTIM/CHILD** will tend to feel **OVERWHELMED** or even **RESENTFUL** in a **CRISIS**.

Let's take a look at an example:

Julie had no head for **FIGURES**.

ALL THAT FINANCIAL STUFF ... BORING!

She relied on others more '**KNOWLEDGEABLE**' in these matters to handle her affairs.

SIGN HERE!

SHONKY & SON INVESTMENTS

LEGAL STUFF ... TEDIOUS!

Of course, it's perfectly **REASONABLE** to seek **ADVICE** from others but making an **INFORMED** choice about the direction **YOUR OWN** life takes is crucial.

Seeing herself as 'helpless', Julie entrusted her **LIFE SAVINGS** without doing **RESEARCH** ...

... only to find that the financiers she trusted had **DISAPPEARED!**

So **WHO** is responsible for this?

THEY RIPPED ME OFF!

HERE'S HER SIGNATURE!

JULIE   or   **MR SHONKY?**

If we perceive situations from the perspective of the **VICTIM**, we will often feel **BETRAYED** or **DISAPPOINTED** because we expect others to look after us.

And when the **VICTIM'S** needs aren't met, the other side of the victim emerges: the **BULLY**.

The **BULLY** may pick on you ...

... or it may **LASH OUT** at those who it perceives have **LET IT DOWN**.

IT WASN'T ME

One of things the **VICTIM** does best is **BLAME**.

The victim's problem **MUST** be because of:

FATE

ENVIRONMENT

SOCIETY

GENES

LUCK or OTHERS.

It's never because of the **VICTIM**!

Blaming outside factors is easy, because then the **VICTIM** doesn't have to take any **RESPONSIBILITY**.

But in doing so you have also given your power away. If you apportion **BLAME** to outside factors then you are also depriving yourself of having any **CONTROL** over the **SITUATION** or the **OUTCOME**.

HOW TO GIVE YOUR POWER AWAY

Donate it to your:

BOSS

DO YOU WANT THIS JOB OR NOT?

SIBLINGS

THEY PICK ON ME!

Each time you allocate **RESPONSIBILITY** to another for where you find yourself, the **VICTIM** has taken **CONTROL**.

And further damage is done because whenever the **VICTIM** feels **DEPRIVED**, **ABANDONED** or **HURT**, it has the tendency to **PUSH AWAY** the very things that it was seeking.

This is because the **VICTIM** has so many **NEEDS**.

It **WHINGES, WHINES, SULKS, MANIPULATES** and **COERCES**.

In doing so, it has pushed away the very **ATTENTION** or **AFFECTION** that it craves.

The victim tends to load **GUILT** onto others if its needs are not met. This creates **RESISTANCE**.

The initial **CARE** and **COMPASSION** that the **VICTIM** is used to receiving by staying in **STRUGGLE** will eventually convert to others':

IRRITATION   AVOIDANCE

AND THEN ...

INDIFFERENCE

I CAN'T COPE!

THAT'S A SHAME.

or even AGGRESSION

GET OVER IT!!

All of which, of course, **REINFORCES** the **VICTIM**!

NOBODY CARES!

To see how this works, let's take a visit to **PLANET VICTIM**.

On this planet, the inhabitants believe that they are **SPECIAL** because they have **SUFFERED** more than others.

WE ARE ELITE!

WE ARE CHOSEN!

The **VICTIMS** get on well together because they speak the same **LANGUAGE**.

SNIFF SOB OUCH OOH AARGH SIGH

HERE'S SOME SALT! WHERE SHALL I POUR IT?

But they are highly **SUSPICIOUS** of others who do not ...

... because they see them as a **THREAT**

> THEY DON'T UNDERSTAND THAT WE'RE FRAGILE!

> THEY COULD HURT US!

So the **VICTIMS** build a **PROTECTIVE WALL** to ward off any **POSSIBLE ATTACK**.

> OK. WE'LL LEAVE YOU TO YOUR SAD PLANET!

But that just makes the others **ANGRY**,

> YEAH, WHO NEEDS IT?

and the **VICTIMS'** worst **FEARS** are realised!

> SEE? THEY REJECTED US!

> TOLD YOU THEY COULDN'T BE TRUSTED!

In **VICTIM** mode, we **NEED** others but are constantly on the lookout for ways that they can **HURT** us. We become **DEFENSIVE**.

The irony is that no-one likes to be treated as an **ENEMY**: this is just the way to **MAKE ONE**!

> A LITTLE **TRUST** OVER HERE THANKS!

And if you **have** been deeply hurt, the **VICTIM/CHILD** in you will find it hard to **FORGIVE** ...

> BUT THEY RUINED MY LIFE!

... which results only in your **OWN** suffering!

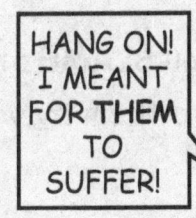

> HANG ON! I MEANT FOR **THEM** TO SUFFER!

WHAT IF THEY DON'T?

> BUT I JUST WANT THEM TO APOLOGISE!

WHAT IF THEY WON'T?

> THEN I GUESS I'M STUCK!

Holding onto a past hurt, you end up damaging **YOURSELF** more than anyone else has done!

> HOW DO YOU MEAN?

Well, when you **BLAME** others, you end up **TETHERED** to them by your anger.

In fact, it is your **RESENTMENT** that hands over the reins to the wrongdoer because whatever they have done or do dictates how **YOU FEEL** or **ACT**!

I'M EVERYWHERE YOU GO!

This also **FIXATES** you in the **PAST** and you then look for even **MORE INJUSTICES** to validate your sense of being **WRONGED**.

IT'S THEIR FAULT I HAD THAT CAR ACCIDENT!

I'M SICK BECAUSE OF HIM!

I CAN'T EAT CHEESE BECAUSE OF MY TRAUMA!

It's a **NO WIN** situation. **LETTING GO** is the only option and it is **FORGIVENESS** that enables this.

BUT IF I FORGIVE HIM, HE WILL HAVE GOT AWAY WITH IT!

There is another way of seeing **FORGIVENESS** and that is:

UNHOOKING YOURSELF FROM THE POWER THAT OTHERS HAVE HAD OVER YOU.

I GUESS I HAVE LET HIM TAKE OVER MY LIFE!

In doing so, you leave others to determine their own **FATE** and you yours. It then ceases to be your **PROBLEM**. Or your **BURDEN**.

OK ... I'M THROUGH WITH YOU! BYE BYE & GOOD LUCK!

FOR BETTER OR WORSE

Can you see how holding onto the past and seeing yourself as a **VICTIM** of circumstances has brought your life to a **SCREAMING HALT?**

Staying focussed on the pain **BLINDS** you to the very things that you long for:

JOY PEACE LOVE FREEDOM

It's not that these things are **UNAVAILABLE** to you — in fact, they are **ALL AROUND** — but your **SADNESS**, **REGRET** and **ANGER** create the illusion of **LACK**.

Because you cannot see past your **PRISON WALLS**, you do not realise that on the other side are all the same opportunities for **HEALING, JOY** and **PEACE** that others have access to.

How can anything **GOOD** come in, if you have **BOLTED** the door against such a **POSSIBILITY**?

NOTHING GOOD HAPPENS TO ME!

It is time to start **UNLOCKING** those doors by learning to see things from a **DIFFERENT PERSPECTIVE**.

I'LL JUST SEE WHAT'S OUT THERE.

Right now your **MISERY** is a huge

What we need do is to **CONVERT** it to a

One of the things that snags us most is a certain **ATTACHMENT** to a past event or events.

You have been **BRAVE** enough to acknowledge that there are certain **EMOTIONAL REWARDS** in staying in the **VICTIM** character. Now you will need to explore the **REASONS** why you are currently **UNWILLING** or **UNABLE** to move on from the past.

OK, take a big **BREATH**. Be **BRAVE** now
and tell the **TRUTH** ...

Do you **REALLY** want to move on?

Is your **PAIN** more
comfortable than
the **CHANGES**
that moving on
might entail?

I SHOULD LEAVE HIM BUT THEN I'D BE ALL ALONE!

Are you afraid
NOT to relate to
OTHERS through
SUFFERING?

WHAT IF PEOPLE DON'T CARE ABOUT ME, IF I'M OK?

How much are
you allowing
SHAME and **GUILT**
to hold you back?

IF ONLY I HAD ... IF ONLY I HADN'T!

Is life more **INTERESTING** when there's **DRAMA** or **CRISIS**?

*GOOD GRIEF, ANY FOOL CAN BE **HAPPY**!*

Does **STAYING STUCK** mean that you don't have to **TRY**, that you can **GIVE UP**?

WHY BOTHER?

Do you even **KNOW** how to live without **HURTING**?

HOW DO YOU DO THAT CURVY MOUTH THING?

If you've never known **OTHERWISE**, how can you be expected to even **RECOGNISE** what being **HAPPY** is like?

*THAT'S **RIGHT**! HOW DO I EVEN **START**?*

Well, why don't we **OBSERVE** a few things that **HAPPY** people do that you need to **LEARN**?

I FORGET MYSELF & ENJOY OTHERS!

WHEN I GIVE I DON'T HAVE EXPECTATIONS!

I WAIT TO SEE WHAT HAPPENS BEFORE I WORRY!

I'M GRATEFUL FOR WHAT I HAVE INSTEAD OF REGRETTING WHAT I LACK!

I'M NOT BOTHERED BY WHAT OTHERS THINK OF ME!

I DON'T TAKE ON BOARD THINGS THAT WEIGH ME DOWN!

Let's get a few things **STRAIGHT**.

> **NO-ONE and NOTHING is going to prevent you from remaining STUCK!**

You can do that for the rest of your life, if you so **CHOOSE**!

If you're waiting for something or someone outside of **YOURSELF** to make it all go away, sorry, but the **BAD NEWS** is:

THAT ISN'T GOING TO HAPPEN!

WAIT!!

HOWEVER, the **GOOD NEWS** is:

> **NO-ONE and NOTHING is PREVENTING you from feeling BETTER, either!**
> **(Other than YOU, that is!)**

Let's take a look at a few other **SNAGS** it would be helpful to **RETHINK** in order to move on.

Whatever happened may have been **TERRIBLE** but the **GREATER MISERY** comes from remaining stuck on the apparent **UNFAIRNESS** of the situation.

UNHAPPINESS is bad enough but we get into real **MISERY** when we:

INSIST that things should be other than they **ARE**

THIS CAN'T BE HAPPENING!

Become **BITTER** or **ENRAGED** because of what has **HAPPENED**

WHY ME?

Sink into **DESPAIR** about the **UNFAIRNESS** of what has **TRANSPIRED**

IT'S SO UNFAIR!

Or **WISH, BEG, HOPE** or **PRAY** for things to just **IMPROVE** by **THEMSELVES**.

PLEASE LET THIS BE OVER!

The trouble with this thinking is that it makes a painful situation **UNBEARABLE**.

We can feel **UNHAPPY** about a situation and this may take the form of

SORROW **ANNOYANCE**

or **WISHING THINGS WERE BETTER**

But we doom ourselves to true **SUFFERING** when we insist that this **SHOULD NOT, MUST NOT** be happening ...

NO! NO! NO!

... and that things remain **HORRIBLE** unless or until this is over.

MY LIFE'S OVER!

LIFE

Let's try a little exercise here:

Make a list of the things that you would like to do that a painful situation, relationship, handicap or history prevents you from doing.

Here are some examples of the way this list is to be phrased:

'I WANT A FULL AND HAPPY LIFE BUT I WAS ABUSED AS A CHILD.'

'I WANT TO BE LOVED BUT I WAS REJECTED MANY TIMES.'

'I WANT TO FEEL GOOD ABOUT MYSELF BUT I LACK CONFIDENCE.'

'I WANT TO STUDY BUT I DON'T KNOW WHERE TO START.'

Do not turn over the page until you have completed the list.

Now, here's a bit of **MAGIC**!

Meet MAURICE THE MAGNIFICENT AND HIS AMAZING ERASING PENCIL!

VOILA! PROBLEM SOLVED!

BUT AND!

When we change the **BUT** into **AND**, a previously **HOPELESS** situation is transformed from something that you are **STALLED** on, to something that you need to **WORK AROUND** or **THROUGH**.

Instead of seeing it this way ...

... you now see it this way.

Instead of having **NO CHOICE**, you now need to seek out some **CREATIVE SOLUTIONS** to get around the obstacle.

Stop building **ROAD BLOCKS**!
NO BUTS!

Whatever has previously **BOGGED YOU DOWN** may still weigh heavily on you but it no longer need mean that your life stops until or unless the painful thing is removed, either **ACTUALLY** or in **MEMORY**.

Because, let's **FACE IT** ...

YOU CAN'T MAKE WHAT'S HAPPENED UN-HAPPEN!

Will **MARTYRING** yourself to tragedy make things **BETTER**?

Your pain will **CONTINUE** if you:

KEEP RERUNNING EVENTS	ADOPT AN IDENTITY CENTRED ON SUFFERING

EXPERIENCE LIFE THROUGH LOSS	ENDLESSLY THINK AND TALK ABOUT IT

BELIEVE THAT NOTHING GOOD CAN FOLLOW  AND IGNORE SOLUTIONS.

But of course it will also **EASE** if you **STOP** doing those things!

A **TRAGEDY** ceases to be a tragedy if it leads to something **GOOD**.

Ask yourself:

HOW CAN I GIVE THIS A BETTER, MEANING?

It's what comes **NEXT** that **MATTERS**.

YOU CARED FOR MY WIFE. I'D LIKE TO VOLUNTEER!

And one of the best ways is to **HELP OTHERS** ... because you now know how it **FEELS**!

The first step to **RECOVERY** is **ACCEPTANCE**.

So, from here on, make this your **MANTRA**:

'It is as it is'.

Give up looking for what's **WRONG**.

Look for something that's **RIGHT**.

Focussing on the hurts only makes them more **POTENT**!

The **NEXT STEP** is to make the **CHANGES** that this situation is pushing you to make.

Then **TRAGEDY** becomes **TRANSFORMATION**!

PLANNING THE ESCAPE ROUTE

We have previously explored the **CHARACTERS** of your life script, now we need to take a look at the past as a '**STORY**' that runs your present responses.

Imagine that the past is a **MOVIE** that runs and reruns in your mind when you encounter situations that **REMIND** you of past events.

Actually, this **MOVIE** is a highly **EDITED** version of your life story.

ENTIRE EPISODES have been excluded because they did not leave as great an emotional **IMPRINT** as others.

Nonetheless, these other things **HAPPENED**.

If your internal 'movie' is made up of **PAINFUL** memories, it means that you have edited out other more **MUNDANE** or **HAPPY** events.

MY LIFE HAS BEEN HARD!

Therefore, you will interpret your past as

PAINFUL or **PLEASANT**

depending on what you are **FOCUSSED** on!

You may **THINK** that you remember everything in vivid detail but do you **REALLY?**

TRY THIS TEST

Think of the pivotal experience that is apparently '**ETCHED** into your **MEMORY**'.

OK. What colour **SOCKS** were you wearing?

What did you have for **BREAKFAST**?

How much **MONEY** did you have on you?

Were there any **FLOWERS** in the room?

This is not to say that your memory of events is **WRONG** but it does demonstrate that we tend to be **SELECTIVE** in what we recall. We tend to recall only the things that draw our **ATTENTION**, thus excluding the things that do not.

If the **PAST** is a **MOVIE** made up of selected scenes from your memory and if these scenes are based on your **OPINIONS** of things that happened, your movie may have greatly altered the original experience to a point where **REALITY** has become **SKEWED**.

The mind is very **INVENTIVE**. We see what we **EXPECT** to see.

TROUBLE! (TRUBBLE)

We experience only that which we **BELIEVE** is possible. We also **RECALL** that which fits our existing **BELIEFS** and **EXPECTATIONS**.

I NEVER HAD ANY FRIENDS!

THANKS A LOT!

However, this process can also be **REVERSED**!

If the past is constructed of the selected scenes that you have **CHOSEN** to recall, have you considered that it is possible to **REWRITE** the past?

- How might you **ALTER** your history?

- How might you reflect on old hurts in a **HELPFUL** light?

- Which scenes might you choose to **KEEP IN** and which might you **THROW OUT**?

- Which scenes might you choose to support the story of your being a **SURVIVOR**, a **LOVING PERSON** or a **GOOD FRIEND**?

- How might changing the script alter the way you feel **NOW**, as the person you are in the **PRESENT**?

And, most **IMPORTANTLY**,

- What scene would you write to come **NEXT**?
- How might you create a whole **NEW MOVIE** for yourself?

COMING SOON ...

```
STORY OF
    A
SURVIVOR
```

BREAKING FREE

EVERYONE HAS EXPERIENCED HURT OR LOSS AT SOME TIME.

However, when we are going through a painful situation, it is easy to believe that we are the **ONLY ONES** who have **SUFFERED** in this way.

THEY SEEM SO CONTENT!

But it is a rare lifetime which does not have its share of **CHALLENGES**, some greater than others.

I'VE LOST MY JOB!

SHE'S REALLY LEAVING!

WHAT IF THERE'S NO CURE?

How else would we **GROW**?

Of course, this will be **COLD COMFORT** to you if you are **SUFFERING** a great deal at the moment.

GRIEF and **ANGER** are **NATURAL** responses to loss or hardship.

I FEEL SO UNBEARABLY SAD.

The way through is to **HONOUR** and **UTILISE** emotions by seeing them for what they are: inbuilt **TOOLS** designed to **RELEASE PAIN!**

OK, GUYS! TIME TO FLUSH!

EMOTIONS SERVE US!

By the way ... exactly **WHO** was the genius who decided that **CRYING** was bad?!

'TWAS I!

AND 'SPARE THE ROD, SPOIL THE CHILD' WAS MINE, TOO. BRILLIANT EH?

However, there is a kind of **TRAPPED** emotion that keeps us in a **LOOP** of **SELF-TORTURE**:

CRYING that just leads to more **CRYING** ...

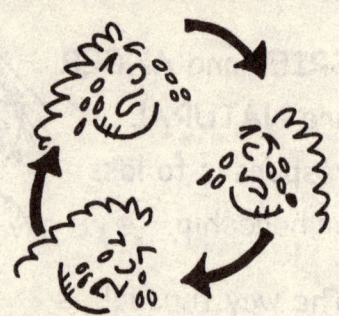

ANGER that just stockpiles into **RAGE** ...

... or festers into **DEPRESSION** ...

... which is **ANGER** turned **INWARD** on **ONESELF**.

A period of healthy **GRIEVING** is meant to lead to **RELIEF, OFFLOADING, FREEING UP,** and **LETTING GO,** not **SHUTTING DOWN.**

Repressing emotions is like putting a **CORK** into a **VOLCANO** —

— it's just going to **BLOW UP** some **OTHER WAY!**

STOICISM may seem 'noble' but it can do a lot of **DAMAGE!**

I'M FINE!

We can learn a lot from
CHILDREN in this regard.

Little Freddie
can be **FURIOUS**
with you
one minute ...

I HATE YOU!

... then **CLIMBING**
on your **KNEE**
the next!

With true release, **IT'S OUT, IT'S OVER** and **NOW THERE'S ROOM FOR SOMETHING BETTER!**

Your **EMOTIONS**
are **VALID**
They are there
to **SERVE** you.

WHEW! INSTANT WEIGHT LOSS!

USE THEM!

Once you have allowed **EMOTIONAL RELEASE**, it is crucial that you begin to see your **TRIALS** in a different light.

True freedom comes with **RULES** and here they are:

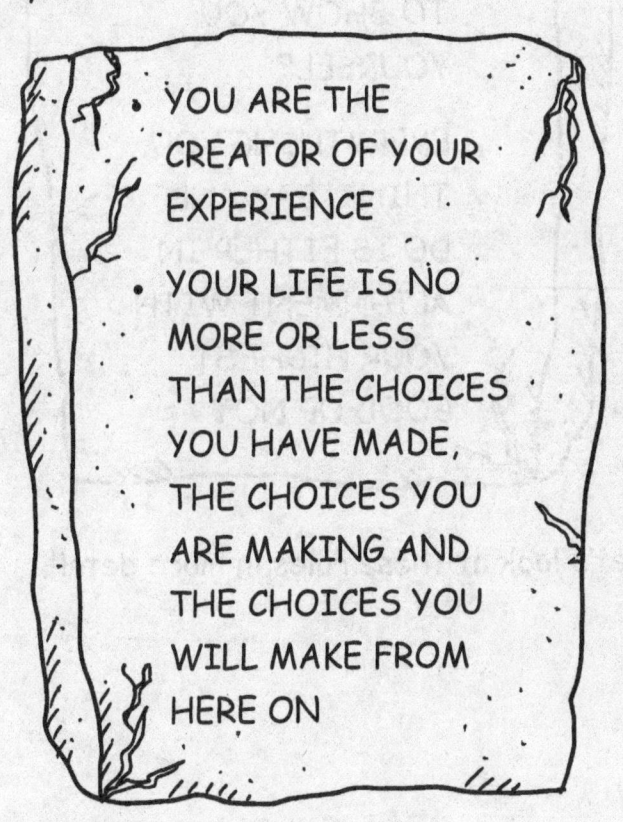

- YOU ARE THE CREATOR OF YOUR EXPERIENCE

- YOUR LIFE IS NO MORE OR LESS THAN THE CHOICES YOU HAVE MADE, THE CHOICES YOU ARE MAKING AND THE CHOICES YOU WILL MAKE FROM HERE ON

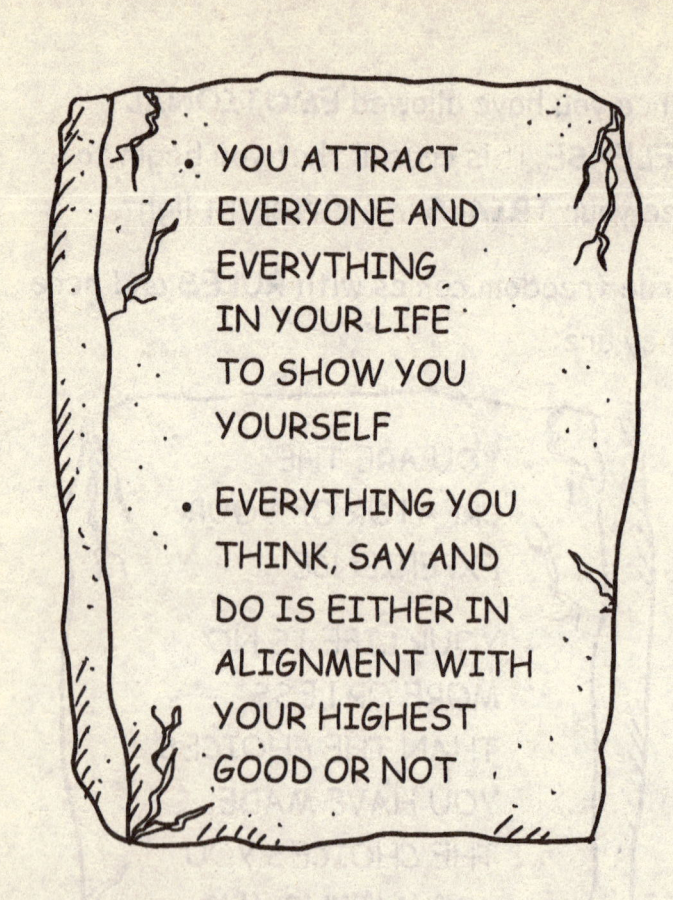

- YOU ATTRACT EVERYONE AND EVERYTHING IN YOUR LIFE TO SHOW YOU YOURSELF

- EVERYTHING YOU THINK, SAY AND DO IS EITHER IN ALIGNMENT WITH YOUR HIGHEST GOOD OR NOT

Let's look at these rules in more detail.

YOU AS CREATOR

Everything in your life has occurred because you chose **A** instead of **B**.

ARE YOU SAYING THAT **I** CAUSE EVERYTHING IN MY LIFE?!

Well, **WHO ELSE** made that particular choice?

Everything unfolds according to the **CHOICES** we make.

OH COME ON! I DIDN'T CHOOSE TO HAVE MY WALLET STOLEN!

Didn't you? Weren't you the one who was walking down **THAT STREET** at the time?

And, by the way, what are your **BELIEFS** around having **MONEY**?

WELL, I CONCEDE THAT MONEY SLIPS THROUGH MY FINGERS BUT I STILL FIND THE IDEA A BIT HARSH!

Maybe so, but how often do we blame **OUTSIDE FACTORS** for where we choose to place **OURSELVES** in life — including how we **CHOOSE** to **REACT** or **RESPOND** to events?

BUMMER.

TERRIBLE HORRIBLE CAN'T COPE! LIFE OVER!

What if you **WERE** willing to take **FULL RESPONSIBILITY**?

How might you then **FEEL** about the things that have happened?

I GUESS I MIGHT FEEL LESS HELPLESS!

How might taking reponsibility **EMPOWER** you?

WELL I KNEW THE RISKS ... IN FUTURE I WON'T IGNORE THEM!

How might you see **CHALLENGES** differently?

IT WAS A WAKE-UP CALL!

How might that **IMPACT** on your feeling as though you are a **VICTIM**?

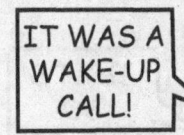

*IT'S BETTER IF **I'M** IN CHARGE OF MY LIFE!*

And there's a **MAGNIFICENT TOOL** at our disposal that we **IGNORE** at our peril ...

INTUITION

Deep down, you **KNEW**, didn't you?

*HMM ... THERE **WAS** A LITTLE VOICE SAYING 'DON'T GO THERE'!*

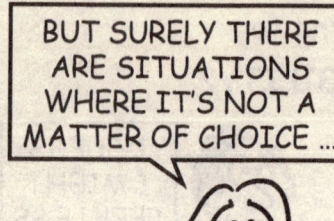

BUT SURELY THERE ARE SITUATIONS WHERE IT'S NOT A MATTER OF CHOICE ...

YES, WHAT ABOUT ABUSE OF CHILDREN, HOME INVASIONS AND SO ON?

THAT'S the situation the child encountered and **THAT'S** the address where the home invasion took place. These are the **FACTS**.

THAT'S SO UNFAIR!

Who says that life is **FAIR**?

If we could control life to fulfil each of our individual ideas of what is **FAIR** there would be ...

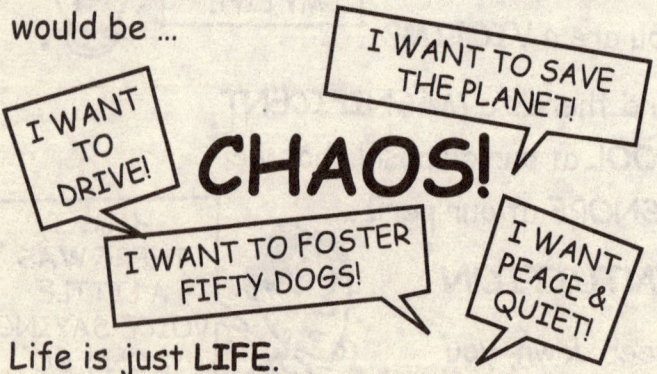

I WANT TO DRIVE!

I WANT TO SAVE THE PLANET!

CHAOS!

I WANT TO FOSTER FIFTY DOGS!

I WANT PEACE & QUIET!

Life is just **LIFE**.
It's neither **FAIR** nor **UNFAIR**.

Sometimes (**MOST** of the time, if we're truthful) we see things **COMING** and sometimes we **DON'T**.

YIKES!

Nevertheless, fairly or unfairly, rightly or wrongly, unconsciously or with awareness, if it happened to you, you were **THERE**.

HMM ... I GET IT — I JUST SHOWED UP FOR THE GIG!

And if you can take **OWNERSHIP** of this, instead of being controlled by the apparent **UNFAIRNESS** of things, you can then start figuring out whether you were there for a **REASON**!

YOUR LIFE BY CHOICE

Put simply, you **COULD** have walked through **DOOR B** but you didn't!

Just as you **CHOSE** to ...

IGNORE YOUR DOUBTS

HMM ... THAT'S A BIT SUSS!

GO THERE AGAIN, EVEN THOUGH YOU KNEW BETTER

I KNEW THIS WOULD HAPPEN!

TRUST THAT UNTRUSTWORTHY PERSON

LEND ME FIFTY?

OK, BUT THERE'S STILL THAT MONEY YOU OWE ME!

SAY YES WHEN YOU WANTED TO SAY NO

OH ALL RIGHT!

I HATE DOING THIS!

GO OUT WITH THAT GUY EVEN THOUGH YOU KNEW HE WAS BAD NEWS

MAYBE HE'LL CHANGE.

TAKE THAT JOB EVEN THOUGH YOU KNEW YOU'D HATE IT

SIGH

And so on ...

For every **CHOICE** there are **CONSEQUENCES** ...

GET OVER IT = WORK
- RELEASING
- ACCEPTING
- RETHINKING

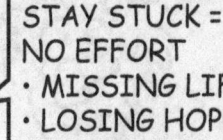

STAY STUCK = NO EFFORT
- MISSING LIFE
- LOSING HOPE
- NO CHANCE

... and for every **THOUGHT** there follows an experience based on that **THOUGHT** ...

IT'S TOO HARD!

... because that's all you **EXPECT**!

NOW I FEEL GUILTY!

There's no need to apportion **BLAME** (to yourself or anyone else)! It's just **HOW IT WENT**!

And since we're on the subject:

- Guilt is an attempt in the **PRESENT** to compensate for some lapse in the **PAST**.
- You can't **UNDO** the past, therefore **GUILT** is **INEFFECTIVE**.

GUILT = WASTE OF TIME/ENERGY!

You might have made some **NOT SO GREAT** choices in the past ...

(BLEW IT.)

... but you **KNOW BETTER** now **BECAUSE** of what you learned from making that choice.

And with this **KNOWLEDGE** you can **CHOOSE** to do better **NEXT TIME**!

*(BUT I KNOW HOW **NOT** TO BLOW IT NEXT TIME!)*

How **ELSE** would you know what works and what doesn't than by **GOING THROUGH** experiences?

Note:
GOING THROUGH;
not **STAYING STUCK**!

THE THINGS YOU ATTRACT

You **ATTRACT TO YOU** the things that show you your relationship with **YOURSELF**.

There is a concept:

> 'If you want to know
> how you're travelling in
> **HERE**,
> take a look at what you're seeing
> **OUT THERE**'.

Here are a few examples:

YIKES! If you're lonely, how do you hold people **AT BAY**?

HE'S SO MEAN TO ME! Do you come back for **MORE**?

I'M TOTALLY BROKE!
MAXED OUT

How do you treat **MONEY** when you **DO** have it?

I'M SICK!

How well have you **LOOKED AFTER** yourself?

I'M MISUNDERSTOOD!

Have you made yourself **CLEAR**?

Can you see how using these experiences to **INFORM** you and making the necessary **CHANGES** takes the **STING** out of apparent hurts?

> BUT I WAS REALLY BETRAYED!

How did you **DEAL** with it?

> WELL. IT WAS HARD AT FIRST ...

> BUT I DID LEARN SELF-RELIANCE!

Then why would you **BLAME** someone for showing you that you needed to **GROW** in this way?

YOUR HIGHEST GOOD

This concept can be your **TOUCHSTONE** for all your choices.

Is it in your **HIGHEST GOOD** to stay **STUCK** in **SUFFERING**?

Is it in your **HIGHEST GOOD** to feel **REGRETFUL**, **RESENTFUL** and **REACTIVE**?

Is it in your **HIGHEST GOOD** to tell yourself **PAINFUL THINGS**?

And, is it in your **HIGHEST GOOD** to remain the **VICTIM**?

Look long and hard at the **POSITION** that you take in life.

What is it that separates those who **OVERCOME** trauma from those who **DON'T**?

It's how they see **THEMSELVES**.

WE HAVE OVERCOME!

WINNERS

SELF-IMAGE is KEY.

We **ACT**   **THINK**

BURDEN — IT'S ALL MY FAULT!

DUD SHAME FOOL GUILT DESPAIR IDIOT SORROW

and **FEEL**

MY OH MY! IT'S MR ANGRY!

according to what we consider our **SELF-WORTH** to be.

If you were a true **FRIEND** to **YOURSELF**, you wouldn't **DREAM** of making yourself feel

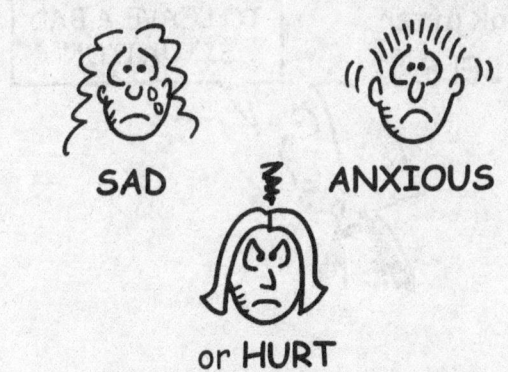

SAD   ANXIOUS

or HURT

If you have **HEALTHY SELF-ESTEEM** you will:

differentiate between **LOVE** and **ABUSE**

BUT I ONLY HURT YOU BECAUSE I CARE SO MUCH!

THIS IS TOXIC!

feel entitled to the **BEST**

I DESERVE RESPECT!

and look after **YOURSELF**.

AND I RESPECT MYSELF ENOUGH TO LEAVE A BAD SITUATION!

In other words, you **TAKE CARE** of yourself.

The **VICTIM** is **COLLAPSED, PASSIVE** and **SUBJECT** to life ...

WHAT'S ONE MORE BLOW ...?

... whereas the **ADULT** self is **PROACTIVE, ACCOUNTABLE** and seeks **SOLUTIONS** in a crisis.

OK. HOW CAN I FIX THIS?

It is time to relinquish the 'sickly comfort' of remaining the **VICTIM**. It is time for the **VICTIM** to go.

RELEASING
THE VICTIM

Isn't it **IRONIC** that, when faced with a **CRISIS** where it would be in our best interests to be **EMPOWERED**, **RESOURCEFUL** and **COMPETENT** ...

(i.e. an **ADULT**)

... instead, we usually allow the **VICTIM/CHILD** in us to take **CHARGE**?

THIS TERRIBLE! HORRIBLE!

WAAH!

Is this **REALLY** something that a **CHILD** should be dealing with?

THE WRONG ONE IS RUNNING THE SHOW!

RIGHT! THIS SERIOUS. EVERYONE SUCK THUMBS!

When the **CHILD** is in charge, you will tend to:

OVER-REACT

IT'S THE END OF EVERYTHING!

BECOME DEFENSIVE

AM NOT.

BLAME — THEIR FAULT!

REBEL — SHOVE IT!

RESIST — CAN'T BE HAPPENING!

or **COLLAPSE** — CAN'T FACE IT!

A simple conversation becomes **CHARGED**

... AND MY CAT MISTY ...

CATS TERRIFY ME!

a difference of opinion becomes a **THREAT**

I THINK THE BLUE ONE LOOKS BETTER!

YOU THINK I HAVE **BAD** TASTE?!

misfortunes become a **COSMIC AGENDA**

GOD HATES ME!

a loss becomes a **TRAGEDY**

I'LL NEVER RECOVER!

and a disagreement becomes a **WAR**.

THAT'S NOT RIGHT!

YOU MONGREL!

Can you see how **EXHAUSTING** and **OVERWHELMING** it is to **LIVE** like that?

The **VICTIM/CHILD** needs the **ADULT YOU** to step up and take care of things so it can **STEP DOWN** from centre stage.

The **ADULT** needs to be the one who provides you with:

COMFORT — IT'S OK!

NURTURE — IT'S ME TIME!

DIRECTION — HERE'S THE PLAN!

SUPPORT — I'LL STAND BY ME!

CHOICE — I CAN SINK OR SWIM! I'LL SWIM!

and **SOLUTIONS**. — RIGHT. LET'S GET STARTED!

However, there is a place for the **HEALTHY CHILD** in you.

This is the **PLAYFUL**, **SPONTANEOUS** and **CREATIVE** aspects of yourself.

It can tell you to:

LIGHTEN UP Take **TIME OUT**

COME AND PLAY!   *CHILL BILL!*

Have **FUN**   Be **SPONTANEOUS**

LET'S BE SILLY!   *YAY!*

and **BE YOURSELF!**

DON'T CARE WHAT YOU THINK!

... all of which can keep you
BALANCED.

When the **ADULT** in you **STEPS UP**, the **VICTIM** can **RETIRE**.

What is the key difference between the **VICTIM** and the **ADULT**?

DIGNITY

Our trials can strengthen us when we give them a **MEANING** and a **CONTEXT**.

Ask yourself:

What do you think you are here to **LEARN**?

> TO ACCEPT?

> I FELT ANGRY ABOUT MY LOT BUT I WAS ALSO ANGRY WITH THOSE WHO DIDN'T DESERVE IT!

How might what you have been through fit with that **LEARNING**?

> I HAD TO LET IT GO BEFORE THEY LET **ME** GO!

How might it **HELP OTHERS**?

> I SEE THE HURT BEHIND PEOPLE'S ANGER NOW. I'M MORE COMPASSIONATE.

Let the past **INFORM** you, **LEARN FROM** it and **MOVE ON!**

Think of it **THIS** way...

    The **PAST** is **RESEARCH**
    The **FUTURE** is **SPECULATION**
    The **PRESENT** is ...
    ANYTHING
    YOU WANT IT TO BE!

What **IS** the **PAST?**

It is an **IDEA**, a **CONSTRUCTION** and a **SET** of **BELIEFS**.

How many **THOUGHTS** did you have yesterday?

They seemed so
SIGNIFICANT at
the time, didn't they?
Well, **WHERE ARE THEY NOW?**

Yes, there may be some wounds that run **VERY DEEP**.

They may take a **LONG TIME** and a lot of **WORK** to heal.

You may need to find ways to **MANAGE** your pain for the rest of your life (and for serious trauma, you may need to recruit some professional help),

but **PLEASE DO MANAGE** it!

And remember this:

A WOUND CANNOT HEAL IF YOU KEEP SCRATCHING IT!

Now, make a list of all the things that **TROUBLE** you. One by one, decide which items are the ones you:

a. **CAN DO SOMETHING ABOUT**

b. **CAN'T DO ANYTHING ABOUT**

I CAN BE MORE POSITIVE!

I CAN'T CHANGE OTHERS!

The things that you **CAN** do something about require your **ATTENTION**.

The things you **CAN'T** do anything about are the ones you need to **ACCEPT** and **SURRENDER** to.

See how far you've already come!

You've moved from:

BLAME to **ACCOUNTABILITY**

THEM!

ME!

from

FEELING LOST to **TAKING THE LEAD**

IT'S TOO MUCH TO BEAR!

ONLY IF I BELIEVE THAT!

and from

HOPELESSNESS to **EMPOWERMENT**

ALL IS LOST!

ONLY THE THINGS THAT HAD TO GO!

Open the gates:

THE PRISONER IS FREE!

TURN THE PAGE
FOR MORE BEV AISBETT
BOOKS

A Guide to Being Your Own Best Friend

BEV AISBETT

I LOVE ME

Do you feel that life has left you out in the cold?
Do you feel unloved, unwanted or overlooked?
Do you reach out to others for support only to find that they leave you disappointed or dissatisfied?

There are times in our lives when we seem to have no-one in our corners, and so we feel depressed, lonely, hurt or angry.

But there is someone to turn to — if you know how. Someone you can trust and rely on, no matter what: yourself!

Bev Aisbett, who has helped thousands of Australians find a way out of depression and anxiety, now shows you how to find the most loyal friend of all ... YOU!

The Book of
IT
Hey, there's not much that BOTHERS me anymore!
10 Steps to Conquering Anxiety
BEV AISBETT
By the bestselling author of
Living with IT

THE BOOK OF IT

Do you beat yourself up over mistakes?
Do you often worry, worry, worry?
Do you tend to expect the worst?
Do things have to be perfect before you can enjoy them?
Do you have a belief that life is hard?
Are you overly concerned about what others think of you?
Do you compare yourself to others?
Do you find it hard expressing your feelings, especially anger?
Do you give more than you get?
Do you look after others more than you do yourself?
Are you critical of yourself and others?
If you answered 'yes' to even half of these questions, would you say that your life and emotions are in balance?

Anxiety isn't a punishment — it's a wake-up call, and you can do something about it!

Using 10 steps from her popular workshops, counsellor Bev Aisbett provides you with practical, sound advice on how to recognise and tame anxiety, whether it affects you just occasionally or every single day.

TAMING THE BLACK DOG

Bev Aisbett

A guide to overcoming DEPRESSION

by the author of Living with It

TAMING THE BLACK DOG

Don't want to get out of bed in the morning? Feeling as though the light at the end of the tunnel is fading? You may be suffering from depression, a condition Winston Churchill referred to as the Black Dog.

Taming the Black Dog is a simple guide to managing depression, which an estimated 1 in 5 people will suffer in one form or another at some time in their lives. This small illustrated tip book contains factual information as well as treatment options.

Modelled on Bev Aisbett's successful *Living with IT*, *Taming the Black Dog* has a unique blend of wit and information and is an invaluable guide for both chronic sufferers of depression as well as anyone with a fit of 'the blues'.